Wishing you a

Merry Christmas

and peace throughout the year.

Blank Classic

Merry Christmas Dotted Bullet Journal
Blue Ornaments
113 numbered pages - 120 total pages
A5 (5.83 x 8.27)

Design © 2020 Blank Classics

Blank Classic

Mailing address:
Blank Classic
PO BOX 4608
Main Station Terminal
349 West Georgia Street
Vancouver, BC
Canada, V6B 4A1

Cover design by: Lauren Dick

ISBN: 978-1-77437-962-2

FIRST EDITION / FIRST PRINTING

— Contents —

Page	Topic

— Contents —

Page	Topic
Page	

— Contents —

Page	Topic

— Contents —

Page	Topic

www.ingramcontent.com/pod-product-compliance
Lightning Source LLC
Chambersburg PA
CBHW050010070726
47598CB00014B/550